Destiny

Destiny

One Hundred Original Inspirational Quotations to Motivate You to Walk in Your Destiny

Karen Danage

Xulon Press

Xulon Press
2301 Lucien Way #415
Maitland, FL 32751
407.339.4217
www.xulonpress.com

© 2019 by Karen Danage

All rights reserved solely by the author. The author guarantees all contents are original and do not infringe upon the legal rights of any other person or work. No part of this book may be reproduced in any form without the permission of the author. The views expressed in this book are not necessarily those of the publisher.

Library of Congress Control Number: 2019902338

Library of Congress
US Programs, Law, and Literature Division
Cataloging in Publication Program
101 Independence Avenue, S.E.
Washington, DC 20540-4283

Printed in the United States of America.

ISBN-13: 978-1-54566-143-7

Dedication

This book is dedicated to my family for their unwavering support and love.

Acknowledgements

I want to acknowledge my mentors, loyal readers and followers for their support and words of encouragement.
And lastly, I want to thank Ms. Lillian Stokes, my sixth-grade teacher, who discovered my gift for writing and told me, "Karen, never stop writing."

From: _____

To: _____

Contents

Dedication v
Acknowledgements vii
Introduction xiii

Achieve 1

Authentic 4

Believe 6

Broken 7

Change 12

Character 15

Conquer 17

Defeat 20

Destiny 22

Doubt 26

Dream 28

Encouragement 33

Excellence 35

Failure 37

Faith 41

God's Love 54

Great. 64

Leadership. 67

Life 72

Love 81

Purpose 92

Relationships. 95

Someday 99

Success. 101

You Are. 109

The Jazz Master Introduction. 111
The Jazz Master 115
Conclusion 123
About the Author 125

Introduction

Are you running from your destiny instead of walking in it? I will admit that I ran from mine. It took me over thirty years to put on my custom shoes made for me by the master shoemaker, God.

I believe the events in our lives act as a midwife to assist us in birthing our destiny and purpose. Without bad experiences, and sometimes excruciating pain, we would never know the right time for the delivery of our dreams. Can you imagine being pregnant for over thirty years?

On December 11, 2011, I experienced a life-threatening event that would motivate me to pursue my destiny and purpose. I was frying chicken for our traditional Sunday dinner when I fainted. I came to and stumbled to the bathroom, where I passed out again. Upon regaining consciousness, I was shocked to find blood all over my bathroom. My family was upstairs, unaware of what had happened. I yelled for help, and they rushed me to the emergency room. The ER doctor discovered a tumor in my stomach. As a result, I was advised to have surgery immediately and a biopsy to ensure the tumor was not malignant. I was at a loss for words; I couldn't believe this was happening. The doctor informed me, in a very matter-of-fact manner, that this incident could have been fatal.

Death had placed its handcuffs on me, but destiny's handcuff key freed me. I believe strongly that this happened because my work on earth had not been completed. It was simply not my time to expire.

The biopsy results revealed the tumor was not malignant. Relieved, I spent several months recovering, unaware that I would face additional medical challenges over the next few years. However, despite my health challenges, I acquired an unexplainable strength and resilience on the inside. I knew something good would come from those dark circumstances.

I had been ambushed by destiny. I couldn't hide anymore. She had never left my side despite me abandoning her. She had been patient and polite. She had done her part as she revealed my gifts in the early phases of my life. Our gifts, talents, and abilities may be dormant or latent, and it often takes someone else to identify them. In my case it was my teacher, Ms. Lillian Stokes, who taught me in the sixth grade at Memphis Campus School in Memphis, Tennessee. I wrote many original stories and poems in her English class. However, one captured her attention. The story was entitled "The Little Green Man," and through it she identified my potential as a young writer. She said to me, "Karen, never stop writing because you have a gift." Her words resonated with me over the years as I have written countless short stories. I have included one of them at the end of the book entitled "The Jazz Master."

As a senior at Los Angeles High School in Los Angeles, California, I was a member of the speech club and student body vice-president. In these roles, I was required to speak to our student body regarding various issues. My speaking abilities were revealed during this phase of my life. I was selected as one of the speakers for our graduating class. The graduation was held at the Pauley Pavilion on the campus of the University of California in Los Angles, California. I wrote an original speech entitled "We Must Strive Not to Equal, but to Excel." My parents had the speech made into a greeting card to distribute to friends and family. I recall looking at that greeting card many times over the years and dreaming of one day becoming an author.

Finally, I could no longer simply talk about, dream about, or flirt with the idea of becoming an author and speaker. I had to become those things or risk having to wear regret's shoes for the rest of my life. The thought of that made my heart race as

I realized I could have so easily left this world with my manuscripts and unspoken speeches still inside of me. I was in the second half of my life. Destiny had placed the ball in my hands. What was I going to do? Take a shot or pass the ball? I decided that no matter what I had been through or what I was going to have to endure, I would stand — with my legs trembling and my hands shaking — and take the shot. I launched my product line, in March 2010, and in 2013, I published my first book, *Girlfriends: One Hundred Original Quotations to Inspire You to Keep Flying*. I am finally walking in my destiny as an inspirational author and speaker. We are all on a journey, ultimately trying to fulfill our destiny. Each of us has a story to tell. I believe with all my heart that my destiny is to inspire and encourage others through my words. My hope is that you are motivated to live the life that was designed for you. As I have experienced through my illness, we must make the most of life because none of us knows when our last day will be.

As you read *Destiny*, I want you to see yourself walking in your custom-made shoes toward your own destiny.

This is a photo taken in 1962 of me as a baby being held by the famous gospel singer, Mahalia Jackson, referred to as "The Queen of Gospel" along with my parents Betty Owens and William Owens. She performed at an event coordinated by my parents. I was born at Meharry Medical College as my parents were students at Tennessee State University, in Nashville, Tennessee. My father often spoke of Ms. Jackson being gracious and kind despite her celebrity status.

Achieve 1

We must be willing to allow ourselves not merely to exist, but to achieve the greatness that lies within us.

Is it possible for our mundane thoughts and actions to extinguish the flames of our greatness? It all begins with what we think of ourselves. I recently read the story of a teenaged girl from Washington, D.C., who despite being homeless, managed to maintain a 4.0 grade point average and was voted homecoming queen at her high school. Her outer circumstances looked very bleak, but the flames of greatness were burning within. She received a college scholarship as well as national attention for her accomplishments.

Achieve 2

Remember that the odds of failing are no greater than the odds of achieving.

We each have the power of choice every day. The choices we make will influence the life we have today and tomorrow. Choosing to achieve doesn't mean we won't be afraid or won't have doubt looming over our heads; rather, it means we are willing to take the risks that are required to be an achiever. It is a misconception that failing means in action or doing nothing. Think of it this way, even when we are sitting in a chair without any motion, that still requires energy. Therefore, doing nothing requires something. The odds are in your favor, so choose to achieve.

Achieve 3

The difference between achievers and losers is in their perspectives. Achievers use their failures as lessons. True losers draw negative conclusions based on their failures and give up.

Some of the greatest athletes, doctors, producers, inventors, politicians, writers, and actors were also the biggest losers. Losing, taken with the right attitude, builds character and tenacity. If you have never lost, you are not truly ready to be a winner. It is the perspective you choose that makes the difference. An achiever resides inside each of us. Don't ever draw conclusions based on losing. Perspective enables you to learn from your failures and become better in the areas that you can honestly identify as weaknesses.

Authentic 4

Don't expect to find authentic friends in a wax museum.

During our family vacation to Washington, D.C., we visited a wax museum. The wax figures looked lifelike. The details of their hair, makeup, and clothes made us believe they were real. They looked so real I found myself wanting to have a conversation with them. However, they were wax. How many times have we ignored the signs of our so-called friends, when in fact they are not really our devoted friends. They look real, but their actions keep telling us "I am wax." Learning to distinguish the "wax figures" from friends will help you become closer to your authentic friends.

Authentic 5

If you desire an authentic life, stop using artificial flavors to enhance it.

I have a passion for cooking, and I believe the secret to tasty food is fresh, real ingredients, not imitation. To live an authentic life means you are willing to become transparent and accept the reality of who you really are as well as the truth of what is artificial and imitation in your life. As you examine your life, you may discover parts of it are more artificial than authentic. Don't panic or become discouraged. Instead, begin replacing the artificial with the authentic.

Believe 6

Fear can dismantle your dreams, while believing in them will enable them to remain intact.

Fear can dismantle your dreams, leaving them scattered like a car that has been dismantled in a chop shop. You must realize the power you have to make your dreams a reality. It is because inventors believed in themselves that they built some of the most magnificent theme parks in this country. I am always astonished by the details and creativity it must have taken to bring them to life. What began as blueprints, cartoon sketches, and huge empty fields of dirt are now theme parks enjoyed by millions each year simply because their creators believed in the impossible.

Broken 7

What do you do with the broken pieces of your life? Glue them back together. You have a lot of life to live.

I have read and listened to stories of survival. Some of the stories were horrific. The circumstances that these individuals lived through broke them physically, mentally, and spiritually and in some instances financially. However, they learned how to turn their pain into assets.

When we use our brokenness as wood to fuel the fires of our hopes and dreams, we become unstoppable. We develop a strength that is obtained only when we have been shattered by life, but we make the choice not to be defined by the circumstances that shattered us. We may be broken individuals, but our dreams, abilities, and future are not broken. Don't allow your brokenness to define you or determine your destiny.

Broken

Don't throw away your broken dreams. They are still attainable if you believe in them.

I doubted my abilities for many years. I was looking at my inabilities and limitations and listening to my critics. I was told more than once, "I'll believe it when I see it." However, I listened to the voice inside of me saying, "Karen, don't ever give up." The truth is, I never stopped thinking about becoming an author. Deep down inside, I still had hope. What if I had thrown my dreams away in the garbage dumpster? My first book, *Girlfriends: One Hundred Original Inspirational Quotations to Inspire You to Keep Flying*, would be a mildewed manuscript in a box collecting dust. If you have thrown aside your dreams, wash them off with some bleach and soap and keep working diligently. They are still attainable.

Broken 9

Courage is not obtained by being perfect; it is obtained by pushing through your fears and striving for excellence despite the broken places that exist in your life.

I have been a perfectionist most of my life. However, I have come to realize I don't have to be perfect to be effective. Don't allow your imperfections, which can produce broken areas in your life, to stop you. If you wait for the perfect job, child, friend, church, or spouse, you might be disappointed because they simply don't exist. I found my strength in having the courage to do my personal best even with the holes existing in my life. Remember, you can still fly despite the holes in your wings.

Broken

Unforeseen challenges can break you into tiny pieces like a jigsaw puzzle, but resilience will enable you to find all the pieces and place them back together.

Life's devastating events can convince you that the sun will never shine again. Like a puzzle, the pieces of your life are scattered everywhere. Because of this, you may draw conclusions or make hasty decisions based on your current situation, which can have damaging consequences for your future. Don't panic! Instead, summon determination and resilience to help you to put the puzzle of your life back together. You will be surprised at how bright your future looks.

Broken 11

Broken people understand how it feels to fall apart. As a result, they never throw away the broken cookies in the jar. They understand the broken ones taste just as good as the whole ones.

I have been through some major challenges in my life that left me feeling like a chipped set of china. On the positive side, this has made me a lot more sensitive to others who find themselves broken. I enjoy reaching into the bag and searching for the broken pieces of cookies or scraping the corner of the dish to get the last, delicious remnants of macaroni and cheese. I have learned that our value is not diminished due to our brokenness; rather, it is often enriched because if we gather enough crumbs, they can make a whole cookie.

Change 12

Not purchasing a plane ticket on Innovations Airlines means you risk becoming a passenger on Antiquated Rail Lines.

When I was a teenager in the 1970s, a certain woman and her family would visit our church periodically. They were eccentrically fashionable — the problem was that their wardrobe consisted of fashion from the sixties rather than the seventies. I must admit I found myself staring. Despite their neat and impeccable appearance, they looked like actors from a movie set because their clothing and accessories were so outdated.

Is it possible to be antiquated and not even know it? If you don't keep up with innovation, many areas in your professional life will not progress; similarly, keeping tabs on the progress in your life at the personal level is not easy. Both require you to assess what is needed to stay relevant in areas such as your occupations, relationships, education, and health.

Perhaps you are faced with deciding whether to stay where you are or become a passenger on Innovations Airlines. My advice, buy the ticket before you are left behind.

Change 13

The winds of change will blow you away if you are not wearing progress's wings.

As I reflect on my life, I realize I have always smelled the aroma of change in the air. In some instances, the winds of change blew very hard. As a result, I put on progress's wings, I was able to make strategic, life-changing decisions, some of which could have derailed my career and life.
It is never easy to deal with change in our lives. However, if we are not willing to be proactive and progressive, we might find ourselves missing out on opportunities and even promotions. Progress affects two kinds of people, those who are planning and enacting the changes, and those who will be the recipients of those changes. I believe there are always warning signs. If we are willing to adapt to change, we will continue thriving and not merely surviving.

Change 14

Refusing to change could mean you will serve a life sentence in Denials Maximum Security Prison.

To live a life in denial might sound stress free or problem free, but instead, what I envision is a life that never reaches its fullest potential or addresses areas of dysfunction. It is like a half-bloomed rosebush or a partially cooked pound cake; full of underdeveloped dreams, relationships, talents, and gifts that never grew as they should have. Removing the denial means we are removing the decay and rot in our life. The rot, if allowed to remain, infects every area of our life. It can cheat each of us out of becoming the brilliant individuals we are destined to be.

Character 15

Character is developed by enduring and overcoming the obstacle course life sets before each of us.

Several of my family members served in various branches of the United States military. They shared stories with me of how difficult basic training was. They endured the demanding commands of the drill sergeant, the heat, the lack of sleep, and the obstacle courses. However, when they graduated, their lives had been transformed. They had all obtained a new confidence that would be with them for the rest of their lives. Their character was further developed not by avoiding the obstacles but by jumping or pushing through them.

Character 16

Never compromise your character to gain the acceptance of others. Remember, people will come and go, but you must live with yourself for an eternity.

I tell my children, "You may have to risk being by yourself." What I mean by this statement is that you must be prepared to take a stand for what you believe in and never compromise who you are. That may mean losing friends. Your character is all you have. When you give that away, you are giving away your soul. People will come and go during your life span, and the truth is that most of them will not be your friends until the end. If you compromise your character, you may risk losing yourself to individuals who don't care deeply for you and don't even have a permanent place in your life.

Conquer 17

You are destined to have a phenomenal life, but you must first conquer your fears. It is time to stop swimming in the fish bowl when there is room for you in the ocean.

Do you feel like a goldfish swimming with sharks? I believe that we can have a phenomenal life. To expand our lives, we must be willing to take risks and overcome our fear of failing.

Conquer 18

Our victories are attained when we refuse to allow defeat to capture us.

Have you been captured by defeat? Have you ever stopped believing in your dreams? When you are faced with quitting, giving up, or throwing in the towel, remember that you are making the decision to surrender, and thus you're being handcuffed by defeat.

Our victories are attained when we keep running despite the limp. Our victories are attained when the tears of pain or anguish are streaming down our face but, we keep working. Our victories are attained when we keep asking for a loan to start our small business despite having been turned down twenty-five times. Our victories are won when we refuse to surrender to defeat.

Conquer 19

If you choose not to conquer, your adversaries will triumph. You have made the decision to be conquered by them.

Recently I was watching the national news. It featured a story of a ninety-year-old runner who finished a twenty-six-mile marathon! The story resonated with me. The woman stated during an interview, that she had beat cancer twice. She said, "You can overcome most challenges in life if you put your mind to it." She made the decision not to be conquered by age or her illness. Although she is ninety years of age, she pushed her frail, but determined body across the finish line. She conquered her adversaries.

Defeat 20

Defeat is a beatable opponent. All it takes to be victorious is to step into the boxing ring and land one right hook.

I enjoy watching sports documentaries revealing how athletes became winners. As children, many of them did not get off to a promising start leading to a future as professional athletes. They were not recruited by universities or chosen in the first-round draft to play professionally. In some instances, they were even told, "I don't think you are good enough." What made them refuse to be defeated? They knew, if they refused to give up, that one day the opportunity would arrive for them to demonstrate their exceptional talents. Some of our greatest athletes were the underdogs. They appeared to be rocks, but they were diamonds. Powerful lessons can be learned from this. We must not be so quick to surrender our future to others; often, it is simply not our time to shine. Instead, we must keep working diligently until our destiny moments come. There are many Most Valuable Players that will never hear their names called because they allowed defeat to knock them out.

This is my high school senior photo taken at Los Angles High School. I delivered and wrote a speech entitled "Strive Not to Equal but to Excel" delivered at my commencement on June 17, 1981, at the Pauley Pavilion located on the campus of the University of California (UCLA).

Destiny 21

Perhaps you keep getting corns on your feet because you are wearing someone else's shoes? God has made a custom pair for you to walk into your destiny.

Watching little girls and boys play dress-up brings back childhood memories. They put on their mother's high heels and their father's work boots, then struggle to walk because the shoes are the wrong size. That is what happens when we try to wear shoes made for someone else.

I envision a warehouse in heaven with thousands of shoes. On the day we were born, God gave each of us a custom pair of shoes to walk into our destiny and fulfill our purpose on earth.

Are you walking in your destiny? Are you fulfilling your purpose? As I have stated, it took me a very long time to walk into my destiny because of the fear of being rejected and the fear of failing. However, it has been an amazing journey. The feedback I have received after my speaking engagements and from those who have purchased my book has been positive and encouraging. Through these experiences, I have learned that even later in life we can become who we were destined to become, and then take our rightful place in the world, filling a void. I can finally say, "I am walking in my destiny."

Destiny 22

You are destined to live a BIG life. However, you must be willing to dwell not in the tiny space created for you by others, but in a place where no walls exist.

Can you imagine trying to live in a doll house? You wouldn't fit in it. Imagine if you were forced to dwell in a tiny space, forced to sit in a corner and not be heard or seen. Often, others will create a tiny place for you in the world based not on your abilities, purpose, and gifts but instead based on their narrow opinion of what you should be or have. It can be a painful experience; you are silently crying on the inside. You want to break free, but the big spaces in the world intimidate you. Instead, you must learn to run with the giants or be run over. You must believe it is your right and, more importantly, your destiny to be a part of the BIG things in the world.

You may have to work in a tiny space, but if you stay focused, your miniature space will begin to increase and expand. One day you will wake up in a place where no walls exist.

Destiny 23

You keep gazing at the mountain, admiring it yet intimidated by its beauty and splendor. It is time to climb it. Your destiny is attained at the top of the mountain, not the bottom.

If you intend on climbing a dangerous mountain, you should first have excellent cardio fitness, doing strength exercises that work all the muscles in your upper body, core, and lower body. You must work hard to attain your destiny. It won't be handed to you on a gold tray; you must go after it. There isn't any fairy godmother to blow fairy dust that will place you into your destiny. You must become passionate and motivated to obtain your destiny. If you don't, you risk looking out the window, forever gazing at the mountain but never climbing it. The time has come for you to climb the mountain to reach your destiny.

Doubt 24

If your dreams have been taken hostage by doubt, faith is an excellent negotiator to rescue them.

Do you ever feel as if your dreams have been taken hostage? You wake up one day and they are gone. Doubt can take your dreams and hold them hostage. Doubt is a bully, demanding that you stop believing in what you have set out to accomplish, holding your dreams against their will. You no longer have a sharp vision of them because you have lost your faith. Faith can restore your dreams. If your dreams have been stolen, allow faith to negotiate and retrieve them.

Doubt 25

Doubting is like having plaque on your teeth. It will make your dreams decay one by one.

For most people, visiting the dentist is not an enjoyable event. However, if you want to have healthy gums and teeth, maintaining follow-ups at least every six months is required. It is routine to clean your teeth during the visit to ensure the removal of plaque, which can produce cavities. Doubt is like plaque in that it can attach itself to your dreams and they will begin to decay until they are destroyed.

We must floss and brush our dreams consistently with "Belief's Toothpaste" to ensure doubt doesn't build up. When we neglect our dreams, they become easy prey to infection. Don't allow your dreams to be destroyed.

Dream 26

Don't unplug the life support machine on your dreams. They haven't died.

Have you given up on your dreams? Left them on the side of the road for dead or barely alive? Perhaps they've been neglected for so long that they are on life support. Dreams are born and, unfortunately, they also die. We abandon them for many reasons — they are too big, they are harshly criticized by others, we can't obtain the funding for them, or we lack a support system to back them. They are still attainable. They may require a good dose of faith, to be given cardiopulmonary resuscitation (CPR). You can bring your dreams back to life.

Dream 27

Your dreams will remain on the ground until you give them wings.

Have you been working on a project, invention, dream, or business for a very long time, perhaps many years? When you began, you didn't have any gray hair. By now, your family and close friends have heard all about your bright ideas. They graciously listen to you, but they are likely saying to themselves, "Here she goes again, talking, talking, and talking about her plans."

Anyone who has worked on a dream understands that it is never as easy as it looks, and it takes time. However, we must be careful not to sit on the runway forever. Sometimes we must pause and ask ourselves what is causing our dreams to never take flight? We must be completely honest with ourselves, identifying the weak areas and working hard to correct them.

It is time to give your dreams their wings, so they can take flight.

Dreams 28

Dreams are never obtained without a fight. Keep your boxing gloves nearby.

Boxing and Kickboxing are extremely brutal sports. Boxers take punches and they also give them. I have seen knockouts. The referee is counting, and if the boxer doesn't get back on his or her feet at the count of ten, the fight is over.

Perhaps you have been knocked out by doubt. It has told you that none of your dreams are going to come true. You must get back up and fight with your swollen black eye and a busted lip. Remember, if you don't fight for your dreams, who will? There is a heavyweight campaign inside of you.

Dream 29

To live life without dreams is like cooking a pot of collard greens without ham hocks. Your life is lacking a rich, savory flavor.

I love to cook and enjoy cooking a variety of foods including Italian, Soul Food, and Mexican. I have a recipe for collard greens that is one of the best, in my opinion. When I take my greens to a potluck dinner, often people who say they don't eat greens have been converted to green lovers after tasting mine. Although I have become more health conscious in recent years, I still use ham hocks on occasion. They are one of the ingredients that put the soul into Soul Food, making a pot of pinto beans and cabbage dance to the rhythm of yummy. If you don't have dreams, your life is perhaps lacking the one ingredient that adds the spice and rich flavor. It takes courage to dream and often requires you to live outside the box, to be adventurous and brave. Accomplishing a dream results in one of the most exhilarating feelings you can know. It is time to add more flavor to your life.

Dream 30

Fear is like barbed wire. It will keep your dreams trapped, unable to free themselves.

As a little girl, every year, I watched *The Wizard of Oz*. Dorothy, the Tin Man, the Scarecrow, and the Lion went on a journey to meet the Wizard of Oz, who could assist them with their needs. When they arrived, they were frightened until they discovered he was not as big and scary as they had imagined him to be. They pulled back the curtain and there he stood, a small man who was afraid himself.

Pursuing our goals and dreams requires resources, skill sets, or expertise that we may not have, and that can bring on a feeling of fear. We may feel inadequate and want to give up. I have learned to ask for assistance in the areas in which I know I'm lacking. Don't be intimidated by others with more knowledge. Often, people are more than willing to help when you are sincere and willing to work hard. It may take a team of people and resources to turn your dreams into a reality. Don't allow fear to place barbed wire around your dreams.

Encouragement 31

Light the warm fires of encouragement. They will keep you warm when discouragement cuts off the electricity.

Discouragement can make you feel cold and alone. However, you can warm yourself up by reading inspirational material or listening to uplifting songs that can melt the icicles of discouragement away. Also, allow trusted loved ones into your life to comfort you during your times of need. Encouragement is like a roaring fire in your heart—it can bring warmth to a cold heart and it can create flames of hope when discouragement has cut off the electricity.

Encouragement 32

Although your heart is filled with doubt and fear, encouragement is always near to carry your burdens and wipe your tears.

You feel as though you have been sent to the darkest place in the universe; you've been put there by discouragement. Imagine if you could escape it by getting on a private jet. The jet would fly you to your own secluded island where you would be greeted by your personal staff—a chef, personal trainer, life coach, and housekeeper. They would take care of your every need until you became strong enough to return home. Of course, that is only a fantasy. It is a sometimes-bitter reality that we must somehow still get up every day because life doesn't give us a time out.

If you are in a dark place today, allow others' encouragement to wipe your tears and chase away doubt and fear.

Excellence 33

Excellence is not obtained by being perfect. It is obtained by striving to be our very best despite our imperfections.

I admire beautiful handmade quilts; the details and the time spent to create them. If they are turned over, the back doesn't resemble the front. The patterns are sometimes not identifiable but are just as beautiful as the front.
If we understood that the excellence we seek is not always going to look neat and tidy, that there is a struggle behind excellence and craftsmanship that most people do not see, I believe that most people wouldn't give up so quickly. Don't become disillusioned or feel as if you are not worthy. The good news is that excellence is attainable and achieved by imperfect people.

Excellence 34

I would rather be captured by excellence then freed by mediocrity.

When I prepare the table or cook a meal, it is done with the spirit of excellence for my family and friends. If you are invited to my home for dinner, you will be treated as though you are dining at a five-star restaurant. I want to make a stellar impression on you. Although it takes more time and effort and accountability, I would rather prepare the meal with a spirit of excellence than throw it together, serving you a partially cooked chicken, half-sweetened tea, and cold mashed potatoes. I would rather make you feel like a welcome guest instead of a burden.

Mediocrity can seem like the easy choice. It doesn't require your best efforts, it doesn't inconvenience you, and it will accept whatever you say or do. The risk lies in living beneath your potential and thus cheating yourself out of the very best that life has for you. Allow excellence to capture you.

Failure 35

The recipe for success will always require two cups of failure. Without it, your dreams will never rise but will remain flat.

I am intrigued by successful people. Each person has their own unique story of their path to success. Failing, I believe, is the main ingredient for success. It acts as the baking powder and yeast that cause biscuits and cornbread to rise. The next time you get back on your feet from a failure, check the oven. To your surprise, you will find that your business, your relationship, and your dreams have begun to rise.

Failure 36

Don't exclude your failures from the story of your life. Without them, your life wouldn't be a bestseller.

I have a small scar from childhood on the left side of my mouth. For many years, people have asked me how I obtained the scar. I tell the story of running into a sliding glass door at our neighbor's house—I failed to see the glass and thought the door was open. I was rushed to the hospital where the doctor stitched the small cut on the left side of my face and a large cut on my left thigh. I have come to accept the scars as beauty marks rather than scars. Your life may be filled with a lot of ugly scars, but you shouldn't be ashamed of them or try to hide them. Your life is a combination of many things, some of which include failing, but it is often your failures that make your life a bestseller. Never be ashamed to reveal your true-life story to others. Use your story to inspire someone else.

Failure 37

Falling doesn't produce failures, never getting back up does.

There are many awards ceremonies held across the country for every conceivable line of work or endeavor. It would be an eye-opening experience if, at those functions, the heroes being honored shared with their audiences how many times they failed and provided all the details for each of those failures. I believe most in the audience would be shocked to discover that their heroes are scarred badly from the many falls they have endured on their paths to success. The lesson-we must not be afraid of falling. It is through those falls that endurance, tenacity, and resilience allow thick skin to be developed.

Remember, life's honor classes are taught in failure's classrooms.

Failure 38

Don't be ashamed of your failures. Instead, place them on your lapel as badges of courage.

Rags-to-riches stories are filled with horrifying details of all that was endured to attain success. These stories include being homeless, sleeping in cars, lack of food and money, rejection, being overlooked, underestimated, laughed at, or told by the experts in their field to pack their bags and go home because they would never "make it." How sweet it can feel when you turn your failures into badges of courage and pin them to your lapel next to your accomplishments. Never allow your failures to define your abilities to become a success or you risk never becoming a great actor, business owner, wife, mother, minister, makeup artist, doctor, professional athlete, or author.

Faith 39

If you choose to be an undercover believer, you are taking a risk. Faith's Rescue Team may not be able to locate you when you call 911.

Would faith be able to find you if you called for help? How would she identify you? One of the hardest challenges, at times, is not compromising our faith. Often, we go "under cover" to fit in, but hiding our true selves from the world is never a good thing.

I believe that we should respect each other's beliefs and faith. The world is like a pot of gumbo filled with many different ethnic, social, economic, and religious differences. However, if you are not grounded in your own beliefs when you find yourself needing faith's rescue team, they may not be able to locate you because you have been camouflaging your faith. Let your faith shine!

Faith 40

Your faith will warn you when fear enters the room. That is why you hear the loud beep.

Faith enables you to accomplish things that seem impossible. However, because you are filled with such joy and excitement as you embark on your quest, fear is sometimes not detected. You believe you can beat breast cancer, your marriage can survive the affair, and there is hope for your child who is battling depression. Or you are over fifty and have just been laid off, but you have exceptional skills and still would like to believe you are employable. Then, just when you think, "I have this," suddenly a loud beeping begins because fear has flown in through an open window. The beep will warn you not to inhale the fumes of uncertainty.

"Get lost, fear!" you say to yourself. "Maybe I won't beat the cancer, my husband won't come back home, I am not too old to find a new job, my daughter will recover from her deep depression." At that very moment, faith grips your hand and reminds you, "You have this."

This is a photo of me and my sixth-grade teacher Mrs. Stokes taken in the 1990's. It was one of the happiest days of my life. I thanked her for impacting my life and assured her that one day I would become a published author.

Faith 41

You can't activate your faith with ice water. It is activated when you face fiery trials.

My faith has been developed over the years due to the fiery circumstances and challenges I faced and overcame, even though sometimes I managed only to stumble through.

If you don't use your muscles, they will begin to atrophy. Individuals who could once walk and run had to relearn how to walk if they hadn't used their muscles over an extended period. If we didn't face trials and difficulties, how would we develop our faith? If you want to develop your faith, choose to walk through the fire and not around it.

Faith 42

Each trial is a test of our faith. If you intend on making an A grade, never attend the doubters' study group. They never take notes.

While attending college, I often studied with a group of students. I made sure they were the students who didn't use the study session as a social hour but instead took it seriously. Who you socialize with when you are facing tough times can determine whether you fail or pass. I have learned to listen closely to what others say. If the conversations are filled with doubt and discouragement, I remove myself. I have also learned we are all at various levels of faith based on our own unique life experiences. Some are at advanced levels, others at remedial levels. Surround yourself with the A students.

Faith 43

It will not be the bright headlights that enable you to see clearly in life's blizzards. It will be your faith.

Have you faced circumstances in life that were so unbelievably difficult and painful that you saw no viable way out? As a result, the problems blinded your vision. What do you do when it is pitch black and there is no light to be found? It is an eerie feeling when you are unable to see what is in front of you. It will be your faith that becomes your flashlight. You will walk through the darkest periods of your life, knowing you will be guided and directed by faith. We all have or will experience blizzards that blind us. However, the good news is that no matter how dark it becomes, your faith will provide the light to bring you through the blizzard safely.

Faith 44

You can negotiate many things in life, but your faith should never be one of them.

Have you ever been so excited about something in your life that you considered it a miracle? I have. I've found myself telling my story often, and I can usually tell by the way my listener is looking at me that they don't really believe me. These events were indeed very traumatic and almost unreal.

Don't ever back down! There will always be those who doubt, but you can bargain to some degree with doubters to win their acceptance. If you stretch compromise too far, however, you risk diluting your faith. Telling your stories of survival should not be considered bragging but should be told to inspire others. You will learn that it's okay when others don't believe. What matters is that you remain committed to your faith and your life stories.

Faith 45

Fear is like a pirate. It can hijack your faith.

I believe fear can steal our dreams. Each of us is carrying valuable cargo within us. Can you imagine a warehouse filled with products and inventions that never made it into stores? Or unpublished books and movie scripts, or cures that never made it to the labs?

What robs millions of people of their dreams every year, like jewel thieves or pirates on the seas? Fear. It seeks out those individuals who are afraid, vulnerable, and unsure. The lesson is that whatever you are trying to accomplish, guard your faith like gold bars. It is that valuable.

Faith 46

Do you sometimes wonder why you have not yet caught a miracle? Perhaps you have been using doubt as your bait.

As a little girl, I remember my grandfather Calvin and grandmother Betty visiting our family in Los Angeles, California. They were avid fishermen, so we took them to Catalina Island for a day of fishing. I recall my grandfather carefully baiting the fishing rod and placing it in the water. They caught fish by using the correct bait. The bait you use will determine what you attract and catch. If you are not reeling in miracles, it may be time to change your bait from doubt to belief and faith.

Faith 47

Discouragement is a thief. But it doesn't want to steal your designer shoes, handbags, and dresses. It wants to steal your faith.

Discouragement, all dressed in black, roams neighborhoods in search of an open window or door to climb through to steal from you. Not your diamond earrings or coin collection—it wants something far more valuable. It wants to steal your faith, which is priceless. I heard a story of a man who treaded water in the ocean for almost two days. It sounds unbelievable. However, his faith enabled him not to drown and gave him the strength he needed until he was rescued.

This can be a life lesson. We can't place a price tag on our faith. It is faith that makes miracles possible in our life. When my doctor informed me that I needed to have a biopsy to ensure the tumor found in my stomach was not malignant, I looked straight into his eyes and told him I didn't believe it was my time to die because I was a woman with faith. My designer handbags and shoes couldn't help me during one of the darkest moments in my life. It was my faith that held me as I wept alone in my hospital room and faith that helped me to wait patiently for my results, which revealed the tumor was not malignant. My advice is to keep your faith in your safe along with your other valuables.

Faith 48

Remember, fear is afraid of one thing; you never giving up.

Fear is a powerful emotion. However, it alone should not be enough to stop you from reaching your dreams. It is a misconception that if we succeed, somehow, we didn't have any fears along the way. It is the ability to keep working, through faith, with trembling knees and unsteady hands that will enable us to get results. It is not fear that robs us of our aspirations, it is quitting that does. When we give up and stop moving, rigor mortis takes over. The hearse called Fear is ready to pick up another dead dream.

Faith 49

Faith is like driving without the headlights on a dark, foggy morning. It will guide you even though you are not able to see your way.

One morning, while driving across the lake in my housing development, I asked myself the question, "How do I know if the bridge is safe and secure?" I have trusted it for twelve years, so I was relying on my faith that it was safe.

If you have dreams or goals, you will need faith to make them come true. If your desire is to write a book, you might hesitate because you're not sure that it will sell. However, you must write your book by faith and believe it will find its place in the literary world. If you desire to return to school at forty, you might not enroll out of fear of feeling out of place as you are in classes with students half your age. However, it is through faith that you will graduate with students young enough to be your children. If you would like to get married at sixty, it is through faith that you will find a mate in the fourth quarter of your life. You will fulfill your dreams, not by sight, but through faith.

God's Love 50

Before you throw your life away, consider getting it reupholstered by God free of charge.

It is amazing to watch the transformation of an old piece of furniture or a dilapidated home as they are restored back to their original luster and beauty. Like an old chair or sofa, periodically we need restoration to occur in our lives. God is standing by to restore you. It is exciting to know His services are free. He can reupholster our battered, destroyed, raggedy lives and make them look brand new again.

God's Love 51

Playing hide-and-seek with God is not a clever idea. He will always find you.

Have you ever played hide-and-seek with God? As I have discovered, the game is impossible with God, for He will always find you. If you are in a sewer, recovery center, mental hospital, prison, or the darkest place imaginable—he will find you. That is good news! He is faithful and loves each of us unconditionally. He will always find you no matter how hard you try to hide.

God's Love 52

God has given each of us talents to make the world a better place. We must decide to use them or risk wondering what our lives could have been.

I was astonished to hear a clear, pristine voice coming from what appeared to be a homeless man. The news reporter had approached him on the street, and the man spoke into his mike with a golden voice. His gift had never left him despite his struggles with drugs and homelessness. His story had an enormous impact on me. It was a conformation that God doesn't break His contractual agreements with us even though we often break them with Him. No matter our circumstances, our gifts, in many instances, remain intact and still are useful. The gentleman was given a second chance in life to showcase his gift when he was subsequently offered numerous jobs as a radio announcer.

God's Love 53

Put your life on cruise control and let God take control of the steering wheel.

I have reached the conclusion that God knows what is best for us. Allowing God to take control can be a struggle. If I were driving, I would avoid potholes, unpaved roads, and side streets. However, I have discovered that God doesn't always use the conventional avenues for us to attain our destiny. We must trust His Global Positioning System (GPS) as He has a planned route based on the purpose He has designed for each of us. When we surrender the car keys to Him or when it looks as though we have accidentally taken a detour, we are exactly where He has destined us to be.

God's Love 54

Having temper tantrums doesn't get God's attention. Our faith does.

One day while I was preparing dinner, I began to think about some challenges I was having. I was frustrated because I felt God was not moving fast enough. I felt stuck and wasn't sure what to do next. I found myself becoming really upset. Then, out of nowhere, this statement came out of my mouth: "God is not moved by my tantrums; He is moved by my faith." In that moment, I felt like a little girl being corrected by her mother.

Reflecting on that situation, I see that I was frustrated and feeling unsure of myself. Sometimes in life we feel as if we are facing a brick wall. We feel as though God has put on earplugs and simply doesn't hear us. However, that is never the case. I completed the project I was working on. When we take a deep breath and face each challenge with faith and patience, we will eventually succeed.

God's Love 55

God's grace has a lifetime warranty. It never runs out.

What if there was an expiration date on God's grace? Can you imagine being in a tough situation, only to be told, "God's grace has expired. From now on, you are on your own." The thought of that happening is scary. He protects us and covers us with His large hands to shield us from the many things that could have destroyed us.

In addition, I have come to realize that I am not to abuse His grace or take it lightly. I should be accountable and responsible with it. I have tried to learn and grow from the mistakes I have made in my life. Remember, God's grace never wears out because He is so loving, forgiving and patient.

God's Love 56

God is the executive chef at Heaven's Café. He prepares and serves love, peace, forgiveness, healing, and restoration.

Where do we get food for our souls? From Heaven's Café, where God is the executive chef and His angels are the sous chefs. Just as our bodies need food to live, our souls must be fed. If they're not, we risk being spiritually malnourished, which means that eventually we die spiritually.

I revere my quiet time in the morning to read inspirational material. This enables me to feed my soul. I want to ensure that I can withstand the many challenges I face from day to day as well as the unexpected. I dine regularly at Heaven's Café.

God's Love 57

Your 350-pound burden might be too heavy for others to carry. Consider giving it to God—He is a heavyweight when it comes to shouldering burdens.

As human beings, we have limits. It is impossible to carry everyone's problems. If you take on too great a load, it won't be long before others will grow tired of you and your heavy burdens.
God wants us to depend solely on Him. God never gets tired of us. He is not looking at His watch or rolling His eyes when we enter His presence with our burdens or issues. There is no burden too light or too heavy for Him. The next time you have a burden, consider giving it to God instead of your friends. God has no weight limit.

God's Love 58

God runs a twenty-four-hour pharmacy, filling prescriptions for broken hearts.

500 milligrams of love

200 milligrams of hope

100 milligrams of encouragement

There will be many dark days and moments of despair in your life; times when you feel as if your heart has been broken. That situation, circumstance, or event was the sledgehammer that imposed the lethal blow to your heart. On the outside, you appear to be okay, but an x-ray would reveal a broken heart. In those moments of distress, what do you do? No doctor or surgeon can help or heal you. But God operates a twenty-four-hour pharmacy where He prescribes remedies to heal you. If your heart has been broken, it is time for it to heal. Pick up your prescription at God's Pharmacy.

God's Love 59

Quit tampering with your alarm clock. God's timing is perfect.

Have you ever felt as if you were trapped in a time machine? Your dreams seem to be millions of miles away. If you could only adjust the clock and make it go forward, that would solve the problem. Each of us has our own alarm clock set by God. All the events, places, people, opportunities, and even challenges in our lives are planned by God to happen at a specific time. When we become anxious and attempt to manually manipulate our alarm clocks, that is when we open the door for disaster to enter our lives. It can be compared to the farmer picking green bananas or tomatoes. They are not yet ripe, but the farmer is in a rush to get his produce to the stores. When we fail to wait on God, we are jumping ahead of Him. It takes preparation, knowledge, maturity, training, and time to prepare us for our destiny. We must learn to trust God and, during those moments of frustration, remember that His timing is perfect, and He is never late.

Great 60

If you begin each day with the attitude of doing your very best, giving 100 percent, when the sun sets you can honestly say, "I had a wonderful day."

My husband has been in the ministry for over thirty years, serving in various capacities. He has also spent a substantial portion of his career working as a chaplain and an administrator with the Department of Justice, the United States Navy, hospitals and hospice care. I admire his commitment. He knows it is his destiny. He has not become like sour milk or lost his passion in performing his duties. He thus remains relevant and continues growing and expanding in his profession.

I believe we should declare each morning, "I am going to give the very best that I have." If we do that, at the end of our shifts we can truthfully say, "I had an enjoyable day."

This is a photo of me at the book signing for my first book, Girlfriends, One Hundred Original Quotations to Inspire You to Keep Flying. I never stop believing that one day I would become a published author.

Great 61

Your greatest days are ahead of you. Past mistakes are like fertilizer for your future garden of great accomplishments, but you must not spend too much time looking back.

I love watching track and field events. In an imaginary scenario, the runners are in the starting blocks with their heads down, waiting for the signal to start the race. The signal is given but none of the runners take off because they are looking over their shoulders at their competitors instead of facing front. Thus, they miss the signal and are eliminated from the race.

Looking over your shoulder at your past errors and your life's typos, mess-ups, and regrets will put leg irons on your potential to have a great future. Instead, use your past mistakes as manure for your new garden called "Great." Manure has an odor, but it is also full of nutrients, and that's what enables you to have the greenest lawn and the best rose bushes. The more mistakes you have made, the richer your fertilizer will be, which means you have the potential to have a green lawn and a great life.

Leadership 62

When it comes to leadership, women have an advantage over their male counterparts. They have an easier time managing the contractions when birthing their vision. They have a higher tolerance for pain.

Being a female in a leadership position comes with both challenges and advantages. One of the advantages is our ability to endure a lot of pain. Biologically, our bodies are different from men's. We are the ones who give birth, which is a monumental accomplishment. We don't usually allow the physical pain we experience to affect our daily duties and responsibilities, including caregiving, cleaning, cooking, listening, and running companies and organizations. We do what we must do—many of us multitask our way through each day. This ability to handle life's stresses and pain enables us to thrive as leaders. It is our secret weapon. Nonetheless, climbing our way up the ladder of what we have deemed to be success is a balancing act. Whether you are the owner of a large business or the director of a food pantry, as a woman you will usually be required—and able—to tolerate the pain and adversity that leading often brings.

Leadership 63

Leading with sincerity produces good attitudes and authentic results.

Good service, good work environments, good teams, good personnel—all have one common trait. The leaders sincerely believe in the organizations mission statement as well as their staff. It is difficult to fake caring, and it doesn't take long before a leader's artificiality or superficiality is exposed. It is not easy to lead, and no matter how hard you try, not everyone will support you or your vision. However, if you have an unwavering commitment to being genuine, your results will never produce anything but authentic group synergy, customer service, and products.

Leadership 64

If you lead unselfishly, you will never have to beg those you lead to give their very best.

Leadership is a honor and a great responsibility no matter in what capacity. It requires that you give of yourself. The most effective leaders in my life were those who led me unselfishly. They gave me their very best even when they faced their own adversity.

My tenth-grade Western Civilization teacher, Mr. Wesley, made the subject of History come alive despite his battle with cancer. I absolutely loved his class. I can still recall the facts I learned. His passion captured my attention and left an impression on me. It was through his unselfish, enthusiastic leadership that I learned to love History.

Leadership 65

If you want to get results from those whom you lead, you must genuinely care — not about their titles in the company, but about their contributions to both the work environment and to the company's vision.

The test of a leader's true character is not in how they greet the company's president. It is in how they treat the lowest-ranking subordinate in an organization. I often wonder what would happen if hidden cameras were installed as we went about our lives. Are we courteous to only the "important" people? Do we speak the same way to the minimum wage worker as we do to the executive?

Every employee plays a key role in the organization. If the person in charge of the coffee makes the best cup of coffee you have ever had, tell them. If the janitors make your floors shiny they look like mirrors, tell them. If your administrative assistant keeps you on track with his or her exceptional organizational skills, tell them. Remember, showing genuine gratitude costs you nothing, but the results your company or organization will reap are priceless.

Leadership 66

Great leaders are not created with ice water; they are created by walking through fires, not around them.

What happens when you find yourself facing layoffs, reorganizations, working with limited resources and having to adapt to various communication styles, and cultural differences as a leader? I believe, when we choose to walk through those fiery circumstances with a commitment to find the best possible solution, we activate the process of becoming a great leader.

Life 67

It is time to conduct an audit of your life. You might discover more liabilities than assets.

When we think of liabilities, homes, cars, and credit cards come to mind. But other liabilities can have the same adverse effects on our lives as unmanageable debt. They might include unhealthy relationships, needy individuals who take and never give, and associating with doubters who constantly remind you that your dream is too big. It may be time to adjust your life's checking account; if you don't, you may risk going bankrupt in all areas of your life.

Life 68

The question to ask yourself is, "Am I making a difference in the world by taking ownership of my life or am I merely renting a space?"

Perhaps hindsight comes with age. You begin to ask questions such as the one above, and you begin editing your bucket list. I am at a place in my life where I want to own it, and not merely exist according to a social security number or zip code. It is not easy to take ownership of your life — it requires knowing who you are and what your purpose is. It is easy to blend into the crowd and follow someone else's agenda instead of your own. If you have been renting or leasing your life, perhaps it is time for you to become an owner. What differences could you make in the world if you owned your life?

Life 69

Becoming wise has a downside. By the time you have figured life out, you have lived at least half of your life.

I enjoy cooking for My Dad when he visits and spending time listening to him reflect on his life. During one of our conversations, he stated, "If I were only fifty-seven again. I would do things differently."

By the time you figure your life out, you have already lived at least half of it. I have always listened to my elders and have used and applied their wisdom in my life. Perhaps that's why I am constantly having talks with my children. I am desperately trying to give them all the wisdom that I have obtained in hopes of them learning from my mistakes. I know they will make mistakes, but perhaps in listening to me they will remember our talks and avoid, or at least be aware of, some of the many hurdles, detours, and pitfalls they will face during their lifetime.

Life 70

A great life is not defined by the possession of material things. It is defined by accomplishing what you were created to do.

If you won a million dollars today, would you still be motivated to pursue your purpose, your destiny in life? I have asked myself this question. The answer for me is yes, I would still write inspirational books. Of course, the money would be a tremendous blessing. However, it would not quench my burning desire to publish. During my thirty-year journey as an author, I have never stopped writing. Through the birth of my children, work promotions, illnesses—my own and others—and death, I have always had a pen or pencil nearby. Money without purpose simply would not provide the contentment I experience by doing what I believe I was created to do—to inspire and motivate others through my words. My mission is to continue publishing the very best inspirational books and to reach as many readers as I can.

Life 71

When we are born, the race begins. We are running in the race called Life. There will be losses and victories. At the end of our race, the question is, did we run our own race or someone else's?

Can you imagine living your life, day after day, year after year, only to realize at some point along the way you haven't been living your own life, but someone else's? A great part of it is over, and you can't return it for a refund! What a tragedy.

We need to ensure we are running our own race. We need to get down to the nitty-gritty of who we are and what we are meant to do with our life. I am amazed at how many people in their fifties don't have a clue as to who they are. Perhaps they ignored the early signs of their purpose. (I was one of them!) Perhaps they were late bloomers who entered their race in the second half of their life. I wish a curriculum could be taught in middle school entitled Find Your Purpose 101 to begin introducing the importance of finding one's purpose in life. However, no such class is taught as a result, I was motivated by my children to write a short story entitled, "The Jazz Master" to encourage them as they journey through life to find their purpose. The story has been included at the end of the book. If we were taught earlier in our lives the importance of finding our purpose, it would have helped many of us avoid the costly mistakes of the wrong career or mismatched relationships. If you have not been running your own race, it is never too late to change lanes.

Life 72

Don't allow the busyness of life to keep you from living your life.

We live in a fast-paced world. It is off to the races as our cars transform themselves into race cars. One morning, as I watched the vehicles changing lanes at a frantic pace, I asked myself, "Have we become so busy that we have forgotten to live? Have we become thoughtless robots, merely following without questioning the program life has placed before each of us?"

Most of us live by a routine because it gives our life structure. However, we must be cautious not to allow the busyness of life to rob us of the spontaneous moments—those moments that often happen when we take time out of the fast lane and enjoy the gift of living.

Life 73

Stop dining with mummies at dinner. The time has come to let go of the dead things in your life.

Can you imagine having dinner party in a morgue? It sounds morbid. However, when we continue to associate with the dead, living things are not able to enter our lives. Identifying and getting rid of the dead areas in your life is critical if you want to have an effective and healthy life. When something dies, it is just a matter of time before the odor of deterioration and decay follows. This is a sign it is time to let it go. Is it possible that your life smells like a septic tank? Perhaps you are afraid to let go of the dead relationship, so you continue dating the mummy. You know in your heart it is time to look for a new job, but you instead you show up every day and clock into the morgue. There are new opportunities waiting for you, but you must first cancel your dinner dates with the mummies.

Life 74

When the oxygen in your environment begins turning into carbon monoxide, it is time to run for your life!

What do you do when the environment you once thrived in becomes toxic? It is no longer providing you with oxygen and nourishment. It is slowly killing you. You must decide to stay, and risk being eliminated or find a new, more productive and healthier environment.

Typically, there will be indications that a job, a relationship, or a business is nearing its end. When it does, it should be apparent that its purpose in your life has been fulfilled. It is never easy to let go as we develop a bond with people, places, and things. However, our lives are too short to waste time. We must instead, get excited about the new opportunities ahead of us. Change is never easy, but when we transition gracefully instead of being forced out, it makes each stage of our life a lot easier.

Love 75

If I knew what I know now, I wouldn't have treated my relationships like trade-ins for a new automobile. New relationships require oil changes as well.

As a little girl, I loved watching the game show *Let's Make a Deal*. The contestants have an opportunity to either keep what they have or risk everything by making another selection in hopes of winning a bigger prize. Is it door number one or door number three? Often, contestants lose, discovering that they should have held on to their first choice.

Perhaps it is human nature to believe that a new relationship will be better than the previous one. However, the shiny veneer of new wears off quickly. Of course, sometimes we must get out of relationships because they are toxic. Perhaps the other individual chooses not to grow or will not change their destructive ways, which means you could be putting yourself in danger. As I have learned, we should try our best to keep our relationships healthy, but there is no such thing as a maintenance-free relationship. At some point, you must change the oil, or you risk the engine in your relationship being destroyed.

Love 76

Congratulations on getting married! My advice? Keep your hardhats on because marriage (or any relationship) is like a construction site. It will require a lot of work to build and maintain.

Think of your marriage as a construction site. Construction sites are not very attractive. They usually contain bulldozers, cement, wood, iron, rocks, nails, mud, and lots of dust and dirt, not to mention skilled workers who put in hundreds of hours of manual labor on each project. However, in the end, beautiful homes and office buildings are produced. Without the construction phase, these buildings would never be created. Marriage is demanding work. It requires frequent repairs and occasional renovations, and sometimes it must be torn down and rebuilt. Keep your hardhats and blueprints handy.

Love 77

There is no greater investment you can make than that of loving yourself. You are guaranteed to never go bankrupt.

I believe self-funding it is the only way to substantively increase your value. Can you imagine yourself walking into the bank and asking for a $500,000 loan to make self-improvements? If not, why not? You must be willing to spend time, money, and effort to obtain the skills needed to become a better person. Too often we depend on others, perhaps unintentionally, to do what only we can do.

You become valuable cargo when you make investments in yourself. In addition, you must be careful not to undervalue yourself. Only you can make a true appraisal of yourself. Don't jeopardize your life by allowing yourself to be auctioned off to the lowest bidder.

Love 78

Tips from old-school love:

- Don't complain if the pancakes are not perfectly round.
- Never move his remote control.
- Don't compare her cooking to your mother's.
- Thank him for attempting to do the laundry even if he accidently pours bleach in with the colored clothes.
- Send her flowers despite her telling you not to waste the money.
- Don't bring up something negative that happened a year ago. Let it go.
- Create a home that each of you will look forward to coming home to.
- If you pull into your driveway and sit in the car for more than five minutes, you may have a problem that needs to be addressed.
- Address relationship issues along the way. If you allow them to pile up, you could be digging a hole from which you can't escape.
- Love shouldn't be based on emotions, but instead on commitment.

We start out with a clean record when we are first married or become involved in a relationship. The crimes of love have not yet been committed. Like a newborn baby, everything is fresh, pure, and innocent. The fragrance of a newborn baby is still memorable to me because the scent represents a new beginning.

However, just as you can't remain an infant forever, you can't stay newlyweds forever. Life will soon infuse the aroma of innocence with the smells of the challenges, disappointments, dysfunction, and hesitation over whether this person is "the one." How do you maintain a union that will endure a magnitude of problems—problems that you may not be equipped to handle because you were never taught about the work involved?

Most of us handle our relationships based on what we were exposed to in our childhood, which may have been total dysfunction. Or perhaps we've convinced ourselves that we can remodel our new spouse just like making home improvements, only to discover that the renovations would require not just paint and a new hardwood floor, but a complete tear-down and rebuilding from scratch.

It is the old-school values that have been proven to work year after year, generation after generation. In the old days, couples kept things simple and maintained their commitment, willing to work hard to improve their union. It is not the biggest and most expensive gifts or statements or acts that create the bond between these couples; rather, it is the respectful way they treat each other that allows them to continue holding hands despite all their adversities. Perhaps it's time for the new school to meet the old school.

Love 79

If you love from a place of abundance instead of scarcity, you will never find yourself empty.

Can you imagine keeping score with the ones you love? You will give your loved ones a hug or compliment based on the number of times they have given them to you. Just the thought of what that process entails is extremely tiring. Loving from a place of abundance and not scarcity requires faith. It also means understanding that those to whom you give your love may not always return it. But I assure you that what you give will somehow come back to you. Your "love checking account" will never be empty because you have already made many deposits that will continue accruing interest over your lifetime.

Love 80

To love unconditionally means to accept the imperfections and inadequacies that exist in each of us, and to remember that most of us are trying very hard to get things right.

I believe we all have a deep desire to be loved for who we are in the raw. That means we put away the makeup and put away the customs and rituals that allow us to pretend to be someone else.

Life is filled with unexpected twists and turns, ups and downs. The people we start out with on our journey might not be there until the end. As I wrestle with accepting my own immortality, which for me means life does have a beginning and an end, I am more focused on the quality of my relationships rather than the quantity. I am also more focused on the good qualities of those individuals in my life. None of us has it all together, but time and maturity can often bring a deeper understanding and appreciation of each other. The time we have on this planet should be used wisely, and when we recognize that most people are trying very hard in their own way to get things right, it becomes much easier to love them (as well as ourselves) despite their imperfections.

Love 81

You can't invite love to come in if you have a "Do Not Disturb" sign hanging over your heart.

If you have ever stayed at a hotel, you have seen the "Do Not Disturb" sign hanging on the doorknob of the guests' rooms. It is there to let staff know when a guest does not want to be disturbed, and the housekeeping department will skip the room if its sign is turned outward. Is it possible that love has not found you yet because you have placed the sign over your heart? This can be complicated, depending on your history. Perhaps you grew up in a home where you didn't receive affection. As a result, you don't know how to give it. Perhaps you have abandonment issues because you were not raised by your maternal father or mother. Perhaps the man or woman in your life is constantly showing you and telling you they love you, but the sign remains over your heart. They become tired of trying to love a person who can't love them back, and eventually, they make the decision to leave. The very thing you feared has come upon you. If you have the sign covering your heart, it is time to ask why. The good news is there is hope. It may require getting some professional counseling, but you must learn to believe that you are worth being loved. It is time to remove the sign.

Love 82

New-school love serves Captain Crunch cereal three times a day. Old-school love understands you must eat oatmeal as well because a sugar high won't last forever.

Puppy love is precious. It has not been tainted by the realities of life yet. These include bills, sickness, broken expectations, and dysfunctional traits that were not revealed during the courtship. You really believe love is enough to pay the bills. But those of us who have lived long enough, understand that the sugar high won't last forever. Maintaining a deep, loving union is one of the most difficult things you will do in life. Many people will enter the race; unfortunately, very few will cross the finish line as a couple. Love requires balance; it requires give and take. It will demand that you still love even when you don't feel like it. You may want to eat the sweet cereal three times a day or live on an island with a beachfront view, but mature, realistic couples understand that true love can withstand both sweet days and bitter ones.

Love 83

If I could love you again, I would catch a star and place it on your head to prove to the world my love for you is the best that I have. Forgive me for not telling you and showing you how much I loved you. I will admit, I took you for granted. I am asking you to please give me a second chance. I want to place a star on your head, because this time I will not let you go.

As I reflect on my marriage, I realize what an amazing journey it has been. We have climbed mountains, road roller coasters, dug ditches, and made many repairs to our thirty-four-year union. I have learned that perfect couples don't exist and that we all make mistakes. Most of us don't have a clue of what we are getting into at the outset. Like lost hikers in the woods, my husband and I were without a compass, but with hard work and a lot of grace and forgiveness we have become better individuals, having each acquired a deeper understanding of our relationship. Most people make plenty of mistakes during their marriage. With regret, in their deepest thoughts, they often wish for a chance to start over. If you find yourself with that second opportunity, make a commitment this time to place a star on your spouse's head.

Purpose 84

Finding your purpose is like discovering a diamond mine. It will enrich your life for a lifetime.

Our gifts and talents often lead us into a hobby, then an occupation, and a business that in turn produces income. It is sometimes easier said than done. However, if we seek purpose and not money, our lives will have more meaning. I believe most of us have a deep desire to make a difference in the world and not just drift like a ship in the ocean without a sail. Knowing your purpose allows you to live a life with direction, and your decisions will reflect that. When you find your purpose, you will discover your own personal diamond mine.

It was an honor and privilege to be the featured speaker at Zig Ziglar, Incorporated, in Plano, Texas. This is a photo of me standing in front of the famous pump. Zig Ziglar the world-famous motivational speaker explains success in life by using the analogy of the water pump.

Purpose 85

Purpose is like a compass, it will help navigate your way through life's wilderness.

When we wake up each day with purpose I believe it enables us to live a more effective and efficient life. As I reflect on my own life's journey, I at times felt like I was lost in life's' wildness. This was a result of me not fully understanding my purpose, which resulted in me wasting time and resources on things that I should not have been involved with. However, I am glad that it is never too late to discover your purpose and then live it as I am currently doing. It takes courage to admit that you might have been lost in life's forest in your thirties, forties or fifties but don't allow that to keep you from pursuing your purpose.

Relationships 86

Putting hair extensions, lipstick, false eyelashes, and stilettos on a "pig" won't change its character or nature. They are going to end up in the mud regardless of your clean-up efforts. If you are an eagle, you don't belong in the mud with the pigs. You belong in the sky, flying high.

It is a scientific fact that pigs have no sweat glands, so they roll in the mud to cool down and to avoid getting sunburned. This means no matter how you attempt to dress them up, they will still end up in the mud. It is their nature. Eagles, on the other hand, live in the forest and spend a great deal of time in the sky, so it's unlikely you will ever find an eagle hanging out with a pig.

The lesson? We must never compromise who we are to fit in. The world is filled with billions of human beings from diverse cultures, socio-economic backgrounds, and ethnic groups, each of which has its own belief systems, goals, and dreams. It is important to find those individuals who are on your level. It doesn't mean you are better than pigs, but they can't relate to you flying in the sky because that is not their natural habitat, and vice versa. If you did try to join them, you'd risk getting your wings stuck in the mud and unable to fly. In relationships, never compromise who you are.

Relationships 87

If you find yourself always turning down your light because others are telling you it is too bright, perhaps it's time to find new friends who use thousand-watt bulbs.

Is it possible your light is shining so brightly that your friends put on their sunglasses when you enter the room? If you find yourself changing and dimming your light just so your friends won't be blinded, perhaps it's time to leave those old friends in the shadows and find a new group of friends whose light is as bright as yours. Perhaps you have outgrown them, or you have decided you are ready to live on a higher level, one where your light continues to become brighter and brighter. Allow yourself to move on. It is not worth losing yourself or your future by changing to a lower-wattage bulb.

Relationships 88

You can't find healthy relationships in life's Emergency Departments.

If you have ever been in a busy emergency room, you know it can be very stressful. Patients there are traumatically injured or ill, which can include loss of blood, screaming, moaning, and a great deal of pain. It is not a healthy environment for healthy relationships. Is it possible to be attracted to those who seem to constantly dwell in life's emergency rooms? Is it possible to nurture and grow a relationship with a person who is infected with negativity, continually unhappy, and codependent — someone who needs drama twenty-four hours a day, and if they don't have a problem they will manufacture one? If you regularly find yourself in the ER, it may be time to ask why. Perhaps you are attracted to patients in the Emergency Department because you yourself are sick. If you want to heal, you must abandon any diseased relationships and head to the recovery room. It is time to be released from the hospital.

Someday 89

Turn your someday into today.

My grandmother, Charlotte, and I would often sit in her cozy kitchen, discussing a wide variety of topics. She loved beautiful items for herself and her house. She would frequently make statements such as, "Someday I am going to replace the sofa in my living room." She always wanted her home to look its very best.

When I reflect on those conversations with my grandmother, I think about the wisdom I have gained from them. I have learned to be careful not to have those types of conversations without also making sure I produce tangible results. While it is positive to speak and dream about our dreams and desires, we must ensure that we are turning them into a reality and not merely having a conversation. As the saying goes, "talk is cheap"; action is what matters in the end. Be a person of action.

Someday 90

Someday and Procrastination are best friends. They share a common goal; they have no intention of ever accomplishing their goals.

Sometimes nothing feels better than to sit by a warm fire and daydream while you sip a good cup of freshly brewed coffee. You may indulge in reflections and reminiscences about life, and perhaps about what you have accomplished and what you have not. Someday is like a sedative. It can slow you down, and before you know it twenty years have passed, and you realize you never did achieve your goal.

But I have good news for you — it is never too late. I am living proof as it took me over thirty years to publish my first book. Sometimes I wish I had done it years earlier, but clearly the time was just not right for me back then. Realistically assess your goals and be honest with yourself — are you procrastinating? If so, don't delay — start making your goals a reality not someday, but today.

Success 91

Keep a pair of sunglasses handy. You don't want the bright lights of success to blind you.

Lights, camera, action! That's what the director says on a movie set, and those words come with all the excitement of success in the making, and hopefully stardom. But if you've ever been on a movie set, you'll know the lights can be very bright and hot. They can also be blinding, making it very hard for you to see what is directly in front of you.
Several years ago, I was in the airport in Atlanta, Georgia. I noticed a celebrity who was the actor in a sitcom that my son and I had watched when he approximately ten years old. When I approached her to and asked for her autograph, I found her to be very pleasant. She was not caught up in her celebrity. Many years would pass before I once again met her at a book signing. I told her my story of meeting her in the Atlanta airport. She is an even bigger celebrity now, but she still has the same gentle spirit. Once you have reached your dreams, be careful not to allow the bright lights of success to blind you. Staying grounded will help you avoid becoming a falling star.

Success 92

Successful people see their obstacles as mere speed bumps along the road. The bumps may slow them down, but they won't stop them.

What are the traits that make successful people successful? One of them is their vision. They don't see obstacles as adversity but as temporary interruptions. Perhaps it is taking you longer than you wish to become a homeowner, to have your first child, or to find your purpose in life. I believe many of us give up too soon, allowing the obstacles to keep us from attaining our maximum potential. Treat obstacles as mere interruptions on your journey to success and you will reach your destination much more quickly.

Success 93

We must learn to applaud the process of attaining success, not just the prize at the end of the journey.

When we observe other people's success stories, it can often appear as though they achieved their goals with ease. They became great and successful overnight, and they made it happen without much effort at all. We honor them with awards accolades, and cheers.

However, the process is somehow left out of these accolades. Without the process, there would be no prize. The process is what enables each of us to become what we were destined to be. Too often you may want to skip to the front of the line, but it is during the times of uncertainty—working long hours, getting back up when you have been knocked down over and over, or being told "no" a million times and crying yourself to sleep—that you reach your prize or destination. Remember, there is a prize to obtain only after we first go through the arduous process of reaching it.

Success 94

Success will not be obtained in sunny dry places but rather in damp places with a lot of rain.

I am convinced that to attain success, you must be willing to work in dark, dirty, damp, and cold places, and often alone. It will not be pretty or neat. It may seem unfair or difficult and will often be the opposite of what you think. Are you willing to do whatever will be required of you to achieve your dreams? If you are willing, then you are ready to succeed.

Success 95

Remember success will not be attained without liabilities; be prepared to manage the losses.

Take a moment and think about your own successes. What are the assets and liabilities? Perhaps you own a successful business and took out a second mortgage to start it. You managed to send all your children to college by working three jobs. You became a successful chef in the restaurant you own, where you started out as a server.

Why do many of us want to avoid looking at the dark side of success? We want to desperately believe in a Success Fairy who is flying around the world and making our dreams come true. But success comes with many liabilities that can include losing friends who slowly disappear as you start making a profit in your business. Perhaps even your best friend became intimidated when you chose to reinvent your career and you're now earning a six-figure income. The key to maintaining success is learning how to manage its liabilities as well as its assets.

Success 96

You can't purchase success at a consignment shop. You must be willing to pay full price.

Everyone loves a good deal and a discount. Bargain shoppers use coupons to save hundreds of dollars on their grocery bill. But you can't use coupons or shop at a discount store to purchase success. It is never going to be marked down. It will always demand full price.

While their success may look glamorous and easily won, be assured that those who have succeeded have paid the full price. Many of them have risked all they had to make their dreams become a reality. If their journeys were made into movies or novels, no doubt they would contain some horror scenes. They would also contain a lot of pain, disappointment, rejection, doubt, and heart ache. That is why you will never be able to purchase success on the clearance rack.

Success 97

Smelling the fragrance of success is good, but eating it is much better.

Most women love to shop. Can you imagine getting only a whiff of designer shoes, dresses, and handbags, but never making a purchase? Walking into a bakery filled with an assortment of freshly baked items, only to stand there taking in the aroma? That would be torture for me because I love to eat! We must allow ourselves not only to smell success but to live it, own it, and enjoy it. It is time to take a bite out of success's donut.

Success 98

Success doesn't require an explanation; however, you will be asked why you didn't try.

You started out baking cakes, cookies, and pies in your small kitchen, and now you own a successful bakery. You used your garage as a warehouse to take orders for your clothing line, and now your customers can purchase your items in various retail stores and online. You were willing to try, to keep working despite the obstacles, and you now reap the benefits.

Success will never ask you to explain yourself to others; obviously, you did something positive or you wouldn't have produced anything. However, if you don't even try, some people may question why. I would rather try and fail than never try at all. Can you live with "what if"? Challenge yourself to try. The worst that can happen is that you will fail and need to try again—which will make your chances of future success that much greater.

You Are 99

You are destined to do so much more with your life, but your garden will never produce the fruits of your labor until you remove the weeds called Dream Killers.

What insects are eating away your garden of dreams? I have an answer; they are the Dream Killers. Initially they will give you a hundred reasons why you won't succeed. But beware! They will be the first to tell you your idea sounds crazy. They are not the cheerleaders at the game but are constantly booing as you make three-point shots. It is time to get rid of the weeds or you risk losing everything that you have planted and worked so hard to nurture, grow, and make flourish.

You Are 100

Perhaps the sun has not shinned for a long time in your life and disappointment has become your companion. Never forget that hope is knocking at your door with a gift basket filled with encouragement, love, peace, and faith.

At times in my life, I have had to hold on to hope like a little girl squeezing her favorite doll. I am always amazed when after some of the most powerful rainstorms; a rainbow makes its appearance. It is a sign to me that there is hope in every dark situation or circumstance. Of course, it is not easy when you are living in the dark, loving in the dark, believing in the dark, eating in the dark, and working in the dark. When you lose hope, you are in a dangerous place; you become vulnerable and begin believing things will never get better. But there is good news! Hope is knocking at your door. If you'll only let her in, you'll see that she has a gift basket just for you.

The Jazz Master

By: Karen Danage

Introduction

My children Maurice, Deylon, and Kayla inspired me to write The Jazz Master. The Jazz Master is a short story about never giving up, finding your purpose, believing in your abilities and never comparing yourself to others. I tell my children they should never attempt to wear someone else's shoes because God made a custom pair just for them to walk into their destiny.

No matter how young or old our children are, they will always be our little boys and girls. As parents, it can be painful to watch them struggle as they attempt to navigate their way through life. Often, they suffer silently with their insecurities which are compounded by societal pressures. I believe every child is created with talents that will enable them to make a difference in the world and to live a life with purpose from infancy to adult hood.

As I reflect on my own childhood, I was unaware of my God given talents and abilities. As a result, I pursued my dreams later rather than earlier in my life. However, my sixth-grade teacher Mrs. Stokes played a vital role in my life as she identified my gift for writing. She stressed the importance of working hard and never giving up. It appeared my destiny had been derailed, but the eleven-year-old girl with pony tails that Mrs. Stokes believed in never stop believing in herself. This impacted me as a parent as I discovered the power of being mentored. I credit Mrs. Stokes with me becoming the author I am today. Therefore, as parents, I believe we play a major role in helping our children discover their destiny and purpose then equipping them to live it. I believe if we turn those moments of rejection into lessons and become transparent by sharing our own failures along with our accomplishments, I believe that our children will understand that success and failure often stand side by side.

I hope that you are inspired by the Jazz Master and will share this story with your children, grandchildren, and others.

– Karen

My family has provided me with the support needed to keep plunging away at my dreams. I am blessed to have them.

This is a photo of our oldest son, with his beautiful wife and our precious grandkids.

The Jazz Master

By: Karen Danage

The walk home from school seemed to take Kayla forever. She thought to herself, "I just want to get home as fast as I can." When Kayla opened the front door, her Grandad, Willie, greeted her with his contagious smile and warm hug and announced, "there are homemade chocolate chip cookies in the kitchen." Kayla didn't make eye contact and stated with her head down, that she was not hungry. She opened her bedroom door and took a deep breath, put her saxophone on her desk and starred at it with disappointment. They were a team that had practiced for hours; however, they were not selected for the band. She wiped her saxophone with her blue velvet cloth and gently placed it in its case. The Booker T Washington High School marching band was very prestigious. Their black uniforms were trimmed in brilliant gold, and they looked like Roman gladiators when they performed.

"Knock, knock, may I come in?" Her Granddad asked. "How was school today?" "It was ok," she said with gloom. "How did the band auditions go?" Kayla slowly lifted her head and stated, with tears streaming down her face, "I was not selected, and I am obviously not good enough." Her Grandfather gave her a big bear hug as he wiped her tears, he said, "Kayla, it is ok to fail. Some of the most successful people have the most scarred up knees. Quitting is not an option young lady. I would have never finished law school if I had given up. I studied hard and was determined to become an attorney. Kayla, you said that you plan on pursuing a career in medicine. You must be willing to work hard to make all of your dreams come true." Grandad Willie reached for her black, berry scented, marker and wrote the word forge on a clean crisp white notebook paper. "I want you to remember the word FORGE when you feel like giving up. The F stands for faith. The O stands for Opportunity. The R stands for Resilience. The G stands for Greatness and the E stands or Excellence." Kayla slowly raised her head to make eye contact with her Granddad and wiped her tears with her sleeve.

"Kayla I would like to tell you a story about my life as a young man. It was the summer of 1962. That year was one of the best years of my life because I met your grandmother, Betty. I was going to law school and worked at Calvin's Ice Cream Parlor to help pay my tuition. It was a sizzling summer day and in walked the most beautiful woman that I had ever seen in my life. She looked like an Egyptian Queen, with high cheek bones, eyes as black as midnight and teeth as white as pearls. She ordered our Friday special which was a cheese burger with fries and a milk shake. I introduced myself and she told me her name was Betty Ann Davis, like the movie star. My knees were shaking but I managed to ask her for her phone number. We met and talked for hours. She was studying to become a nurse and we discovered we both had a passion for music. I told her that I played the saxophone.

She invited me to meet her uncle at the Cotton Club in Harlem, New York. They were rehearsing as we entered the club the sound that was coming from the band was magical. Her uncle was the famous, 'Jazz Master.' He was the best! He made a saxophone talk, as the old folks would say. Which meant he was exceptional. He was a tall, classy gentleman and his suits were as elegant as his speech. I had an opportunity to audition for his band and was selected on the third attempt. I practiced, practiced, and practiced until there were blisters on my fingers and I was not selected on my first attempt. I was devasted but decided not to give up. The Jazz Master told me, when you play from the heart it reaches the heart. When I began to play from the heart and believed in my own abilities, my performances improved and as a result I was selected for the band. Kayla, I can help you practice, but you must be patient, persistent, and most importantly, believe. Kayla felt relived and took a deep breath. She decided to work hard for the next six months and audition again.

She walked briskly from school and was excited about practicing with her Granddad. She opened the door, washed her hands, and began eating the freshly baked chocolate chip cookies that were still warm. "How was school her Granddad asked?" "It was good she stated with a smile."
"Are you ready to practice?" She finished chewing her cookie and took a sip of cold milk and then said, "yes!" "What is your favorite song?" Her Granddad asked, Kayla responded without hesitation, "Rise Up." "Ok." Kayla's Granddad closed his eyes and listened intensely to every note. Kayla began to play. Kayla stopped and started over and over. "Kayla, what are you thinking about?" her Granddad asked. "I am thinking about the day I auditioned and didn't get selected and the fact the other kids were so much better than me." Her Granddad left and came back with her brother's shoes, Maurice and Deylon. "Kayla, put these on," her Granddad commanded. Kayla began to laugh and said, "I can't fit my brothers' shoes!" "Kayla, you are correct. Your brother's shoes are not your size. The problem with some of us is, we are trying

to wear someone else's shoes. Kayla, remember that God has made a custom pair for you to walk into your destiny.

The Booker T Washington High School marching band is exceptional because each member wears their custom-made shoes. You will excel when you stop doubting your abilities and comparing yourself to others. I want you to focus and pretend you are playing at Carnegie Hall."

Kayla stood up and played again. "That is much better," Granddad Willie said. It seemed like only a week, but six months had passed. Kayla could smell the aroma of bacon, coffee, and Grandma Betty's homemade buttermilk biscuit's coming from the kitchen. It was a family tradition to eat Sunday breakfast before going to church.

"Kayla, your Mom and I are proud of you." Kayla's Dad, Robert, said. "We have

heard you practicing every day. Pastor Rowe told me you have been selected to perform a solo this morning." Kayla's Dad asked her what her musical selection was? She stated with her contagious smile that it is a surprise.

The sun shined brightly through the windows of the church. Sister Smith was responsible for the Sunday announcements. The congregation looked forward to seeing Sister Smith because her Sunday wardrobe was amazing. This Sunday she wore a beautiful red dress with a large red hat, embellished with red artificial roses. She proudly announced that it was Youth Sunday and all new members were invited to join the pastoral staff and members after service for dinner in the new fellowship hall and they didn't want to miss dinner because Sister Yolanda donated her award-winning homemade banana pudding for desert. Upon the completion of the announcements Kayla, walked up and stood at the bottom of the steps of the stage waiting to be introduced. Pastor Trai, the Youth Pastor, introduced Kayla. She carefully walked up the steps to the pulpit and walked past the pastoral staff sitting in purple high back chairs on her way to the podium. She closed her eyes and began to play, "How Great Thou Art." This was Granddad Willie's favorite Christian hymn. Tears began to roll down her Granddad's slightly wrinkled, distinguished face. He was overwhelmed with joy because Kayla was playing from the heart and not her head. When Kayla completed playing, she received a standing ovation from the church congregation.

Kayla pushed her blanket off her legs and yawned. She thought to herself, it's Monday. She watched the sun rise and noticed a bluebird in the tree. The bird appeared to wink and move its beak at Kayla as if to say, "you are going to do well today." She was ready to audition. She was going to wear the shoes that God had custom made for her and be the best saxophone player. She entered the auditorium and was given the number ten. Kayla took her seat and waited for her number to be called. While waiting, she began to day dream about the practice sessions with her Granddad as well as the dozens of chocolate chip cookies she had consumed. The number ten was called, and Kayla was next.

She took a quick glance at the palm of her right hand where she wrote the word

FORGE. The band director, Mr. Wang, was impressed with Kayla's new

confidence. She took her place on the stage and pretended that she was playing

for a sold-out crowd at Carnegie Hall. Her performance was flawless. The

judge couldn't believe this was the same girl that had auditioned six months ago.

Mr. Wang, complemented Kayla and informed her that selections would be posted the next day.

Kayla felt like she had butterflies in her stomach. She slowly opened the door

and hesitated but remembered her Granddad's words "Kayla, never quit." Kayla

had mixed emotions of defeat and victory. As she walked towards the hall

to find out if she was selected, her heart began to race. The excitement was overwhelming as students in the hallway were taking selfies and shouting, "I made it! I made it!" She gently pushed her way through the crowd, and saw her name, Kayla Alisa Danage. Kayla said to herself, *Granddad is right, it is ok to fail, and most successful people have the scarred-up knees.* Although Kayla never met the Jazz Master, she was glad her Granddad had.

The End

Conclusion

It is time for you to wear your custom-made shoes made by the master shoemaker, God. They will never wear out or need repairs. Remember, the journey won't be easy or without obstacles, fear, detours, tears or set-backs. It is for you to walk into your destiny.

From my heart to yours---keep walking

– Karen

About the Author

For more information about Karen please visit
www.kareninspires.com

CPSIA information can be obtained
at www.ICGtesting.com
Printed in the USA
LVHW040735201222
735517LV00008B/679